The Magic Moon Machine

by Jane Belk Moncure
illustrated by Linda Hohag
and Dan Spoden

Published by

THE CHILD'S WORLD

Mankato, Minnesota

The Library —
A Magic Castle

Come to the magic castle
When you are growing tall.
Rows upon rows of Word Windows
Line every single wall.
They reach up high,
As high as the sky,
And you want to open them all.
For every time you open one,
A new adventure has begun.

Kim opened a Word Window.

Guess what he saw?

An astronaut in a magic moon machine. A sign on the door said:

Leaving soon for the Moon

"Wait," said Kim. "May I go with you? And may I take my pets with me too?"

"Yes," said the astronaut, "but just a few." So Kim took . . .

his pony,

two cats,

and
four dogs,

a bowl full
of goldfish,

and eight
jumpy frogs.

"No more," said the
astronaut. He closed the door.
"Wait," said Kim. "I need one thing more."

9

"I need to take my toys with me."
So Kim took . . .

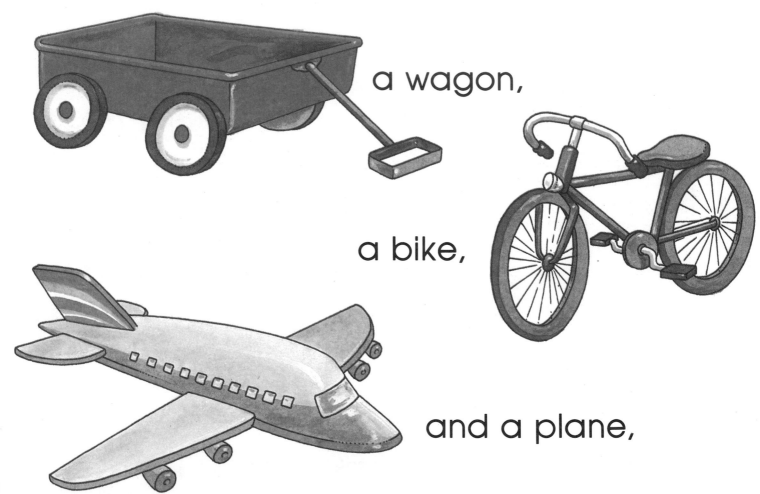

a wagon,

a bike,

and a plane,

six race cars,

one robot,

three balls,

and a train.

11

"No more stuff," said
the astronaut.
"Let's go."

But Kim stopped and shook his head no.
"Wait," he said. "I need one thing more. . . .

I must take some food with me." He ran
to the store.

13

He bought . . .

twelve donuts,

some bread and some jam,

seven ice-cream cones,

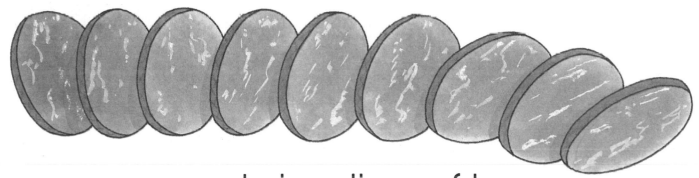

and nine slices of ham.

"No more stuff," said the astronaut.
"Let's go." But Kim shook his head no.

"I may need a house on the moon," he said.
So he ran for . . .

some
lumber,

a hammer and nails,

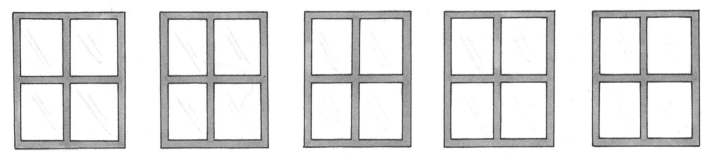

five windows,

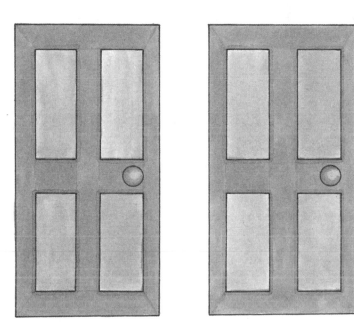

two doors,

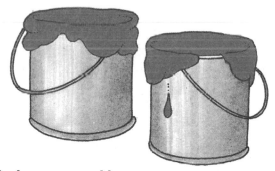

and some red paint in pails.

He stuffed in a table,

a chair,

and a bed,

and ten warm blankets.

"It's cold there," he said.

Then he stuffed in . . .

his snowsuit,

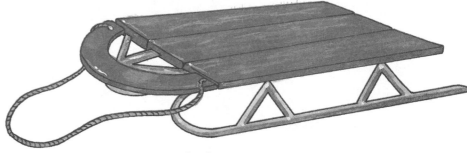

his sled,

and his skis.

"If it snows on the moon, I might need these."

"Stop," said the astronaut. "Close the door. We cannot take one thing more."

Was Kim ready to go to the moon?
Can you guess?

"Yes," said Kim. "Yes. Yes. Yes."

"Count down," said the astronaut.

"Ten,
nine,
eight,
seven,
six,
five,
four—"

"Stop," said Kim. "I do need one thing more."

Kim ran to get a telephone. "While I'm away, I may want to call home."

The astronaut shook his head. "We have too much stuff," he said.
But Kim went on counting,

". . . three,
  two,
  one.
Here we go.
This will be fun."

Did the magic moon machine fly? Oh, no.
Do you know why?

It had too many things to go up in the sky.

"Bye-bye," said the astronaut as he zoomed away. "I will take you with me another day."

Then Kim said, "The next time that magic moon machine comes by, I will take only me, myself, and I."

And he closed the Word Window.

You can count the things  Kim put in the magic moon machine.

1

2

3

4

5

6